KU-213-505

RESOURCES *for* LEARNING *in* COLLEGE LIBRARIES

The report of the LA
college library survey 1993–94

Tricia Hamm
David Marsden
Steve Wisher

HAVERING COLLEGE
OF FURTHER & HIGHER EDUCATION
LEARNING RESOURCES
CENTRE

LIBRARY ASSOCIATION PUBLISHING
LONDON

AG

027.7 REF   17288

© The Library Association 1995

Published by
Library Association Publishing
7 Ridgmount Street
London WC1E 7AE

Except as otherwise permitted under the Copyright Designs and Patents Act 1988 this publication may only be reproduced, stored or transmitted in any form or by any means, with the prior permission of the publisher, or, in the case of reprographic reproduction, in accordance with the terms of a licence issued by The Copyright Licensing Agency. Enquiries concerning reproduction outside those terms should be sent to Library Association Publishing, 7 Ridgmount Street, London WC1E 7AE.

First published 1995

British Library Cataloguing in Publication Data
A catalogue record for this book is available from the British Library

ISBN 1-85604-187-5

Tricia Hamm, David Marsden and Steve Wisher

The Survey and Statistical Research Centre
Sheffield Hallam University
Hallamshire Business Park
100 Napier Street
Sheffield S11 8HD

Telephone 0114 253 3121/3791

Camera-ready copy supplied by The Survey and Statistical Research Centre, Sheffield Hallam University.
Printed and made in Great Britain by Bookcraft (Bath) Ltd.

CONTENTS

ACKNOWLEDGEMENTS

Our thanks are due to numerous people who assisted during the course of this research. In particular:

- Carl Clayton and Guy Daines at the Library Association.

- Rachel Cornes, Dot Biggin, and other staff at the Survey and Statistical Research Centre.

- All the respondents to the survey who took valuable time to complete the questionnaire.

EXECUTIVE SUMMARY

1. The aim of this research was to examine the levels of provision and resourcing in college libraries in the UK.

2. The research was conducted jointly by the Library Association (LA) and the Survey and Statistical Research Centre (SSRC) at Sheffield Hallam University.

3. Data was collected by sending a self-completion questionnaire to a total of 555 Colleges across the U.K. The overall response rate to the survey was 69% - an improvement on the 1991/2 and 1989 surveys, where response rates of just over 50% were achieved.

Profile of Colleges

4. In total, 55% of responses to the survey were from general Further Education (FE) colleges. This survey was the first to include sixth-form colleges, these comprising 19% of respondents. To allow comparisons with previous survey data, responses from sixth-form colleges are removed from the analysis where required.

5. In general, sixth-form colleges and those classed in the 'other' category (Agricultural, Art and Design and Designated Colleges) were smaller in terms of number of FTE students. The median student FTE in sixth-form colleges being 850, compared with 2624 in general FE colleges and 2221 in Tertiary Colleges.

6. Almost a half (46%) of responding colleges described their library as an autonomous department. A further third were part of Learning Resources Department. In sixth-form colleges, libraries were more likely to be autonomous departments; in general FE they were equally likely to be part of LRDs as autonomous.

7. A larger proportion of colleges have now moved to incorporating libraries into LRDs. Excluding sixth-form colleges, this was the case for 24% of colleges in 1991/92 and 36% in 1993/94.

8. Thirty-seven percent of colleges had 2500+ FTE students - these being described as 'large colleges'.

9. Sixth-form and 'other' colleges were more likely to be small (less than 1000 FTE students). There were **no** large sixth-form colleges.

10. Almost two-thirds of colleges (63%) had just one staffed library site. This was the case for **all** sixth-form colleges. General FE colleges were more likely to have more sites - 69% had more than one.

11. Only a small proportion of colleges anticipated a merger with another college in the future. Those that did were, as might be expected, smaller in terms of FTE students.

12. Four-fifths of libraries had produced or were producing a statement of aims and objectives or a strategic plan. Only 38% were producing or had produced a users' charter.

Aspects of Provision

13. The median for floor area occupied by college libraries was 300 sq.m. Fifteen percent of colleges had library floor areas of 1000+ sq. m.

14. The results highlight the expected link between library floor area and college size. The pattern is not, however, always consistent - for example, 5 colleges with 2500+ FTE students had libraries of less than 250 sq. m.

15. The median number of reader places was 100 - an increase from the 1991/92 figure of 91.

16. The median number of reader places per FTE was 0.059.

17. Approximately two-thirds of libraries have automated cataloguing, this figure rising to 71% within general FE colleges.

18. Overall, only 21% of general FE colleges reported **no** functions automated, this being the case for 25% of sixth-form, 32% of tertiary and 37% of 'other' colleges.

19.   The median bookstock was 22,000 in 1991/92 and 20,000 in 1993/94. This latter figure includes sixth-form colleges which tended to have lower bookstocks than general FE and Tertiary.

20.   Examining bookstock per FTE student, however, points to higher unit provision figures in sixth-form colleges. The median books per FTE were 12.56 in sixth-form, 10.25 in general FE and 11.15 in Tertiary colleges.

21.   The median number of additions to bookstock was 1311 in 1993/94, compared with 1310 in 1991/92.

22.   The median weekly opening hours of libraries was 53 during term-time and 35 hours during vacations - these being similar to the 1991/92 survey.

23.   Forty-two percent of college libraries reported 3000+ term-time visits per week. This was the case for 13% of libraries in 1991/92. This striking increase may partly be a result of different structures in the two survey samples.

24.   In contrast, the number of weekly issues reported by libraries has declined - the median issues being 491 in 1991/92 and 445 in 1993/94. The later figure excludes sixth-form colleges for comparison purposes.

Finance

25.   In 29% of colleges decisions about the size of library budget were made by the Principal or College Director.

26.   The median library expenditure (excluding salaries) in responding colleges was £26,411, although large differences exist between types of college.

27.   Considering the ratio of library budget to college budget, the median figure was 1%. However, differences exist by college type - 66% of sixth-form colleges received less than 1% of the college budget. Libraries within LRDs generally received a larger proportion of the college budget.

28.   The median library expenditure per FTE student was £16.66. The comparable figures for sixth-form, general FE and tertiary being £11.02, £16.67 and £14.90, respectively.

29.   Overall, 20% of colleges indicated that their 1994/95 (non-staffing) budget was smaller than for 1993/94.

30.   The survey highlights increased library expenditure in a number of areas, particularly on CD-ROMS. A third of respondents anticipated spending at least 80% more on this stock item in 1994/95 than in the previous year.

Staffing

31.   Forty-eight percent of staff who were in direct operational control of the library were chartered librarians.

32.   Only a small proportion (4%) of libraries or heads of library service were members of the college Senior Management Team; 78% reported to an SMT member.

33.   In a third of colleges, the person in charge of the library was of grade APC Scale 6 or below.

34.   The survey revealed clear gender differences in the grading of library managers - 52% of male library managers were at lecturer/senior lecturer/management spine level; this being the case for 24% of female library managers.

35.   Almost a half (49%) of the professionally qualified or management posts in libraries were on APC Scale 4-6. Forty-three percent of library support posts were Scale 1-2.

36.   The median ratio of library staff to FTE students was 1:433. Smaller colleges tended to have better staff : student ratios. Twenty-seven percent of small colleges had staff : student ratios of at least 1 : 500, this being the case for 45% of large colleges.

1. INTRODUCTION

Background: FE and libraries context

> "*Libraries are often a weak aspect of provision. Many are too small for the number of enrolled students, have insufficient study spaces and an inadequate or outdated bookstock. Upgrading library facilities is a priority for many college managers, often as part of an overall strategy for the development of resources to support independent study by students*" (FEFC, 1994).

1.1 Since incorporation in 1993, the FE sector has seen striking changes. To begin with, colleges have had to gain expertise rapidly in financial control, personnel and premises management, and have had to adapt their internal structures, incorporate marketing and promotion into their remit and to adopt a strong business orientation (Crequer, 1995). While colleges have met the challenges with enthusiasm, the sector has faced many difficulties. The move towards expansion in particular - including the growth in franchised courses - has been accompanied by reductions in unit funding.

1.2 Other trends such as the move towards student-centred learning have also had critical effects on library provision and management. Adapting to this shift in learning styles, library staff are having increasing input into curriculum delivery and thus are more involved with other college staff and students; in supporting resource-based learning too, it is important that they balance traditional library resources with new IT developments. The implications of these developments on staff training alone are huge.

1.3 Despite dramatic changes in FE, commentators have pointed to the strange 'invisibility' of the sector - and also to the low profile of libraries within it. It has been said that FE colleges spend less per student on books and periodicals than universities and buy less expensive items. Yet - if part-time day and evening students are included - at a figure of 3.5 million, they have twice the potential library users (Beckett, 1995).

Aims of the Research

1.4   The purpose of this current research was to examine levels of provision and resourcing in college libraries, building upon areas investigated in a similar survey in 1991-2 (Bibby, Eastwood and Wisher, 1994) and also in previous years (Library Association, 1993, 1989). Like the previous surveys, this research was based on a questionnaire requiring librarians or heads of service to provide statistical returns relating to:

- the structure and position of the library and college,
- stock,
- facilities and levels of activity,
- finance,
- staffing.

1.5   Measures which provided the basis for analysis in the previous survey had been prepared by Fisher (1993). These indicators were used again in the 1995 survey, but were expanded to look at areas in more detail and also to include analysis of some of the new developments in FE in general and libraries in particular; the current research, for example, examined some aspects of automation and library involvement in strategic planning.

Issues Raised by the Previous Survey (1991-2)

1.6   Data elicited from the 1992 survey essentially provided an important indication of the position of college libraries at a particular point in time and allowed some comparison with previous data from 1989 in the areas of library revenue and stock items. However, the data collected in 1992 was itself not sufficiently robust to be an adequate planning tool. Findings from both the survey data and from interviews with key FE sector and libraries personnel at that point strengthened the need for valid and reliable time series data - crucial in an FE and libraries context which was constantly changing and evolving. In this light, particular directions were suggested by the research; it was felt, for, example, that a critical element of future research would be to look at technological change in library provision.

Additional Issues Raised by Current Survey

1.7   In the 1995 survey a number of respondents inserted additional comments about their libraries on the survey questionnaire. These are discussed within the appropriate sections of the report.

2. METHODOLOGY

Research Method and Sample

2.1 The research was conducted jointly by the Library Association (LA) and the Survey and Statistical Research Centre (SSRC) at Sheffield Hallam University. The chosen method was by self-completion questionnaire, with the questionnaire being designed by the SSRC in consultation with the LA. It was piloted extensively through the London and Yorkshire COFHE regional groups with a number of participants completing draft questionnaires and commenting on question validity, wording and appropriateness.

2.2 In the main survey, the Library Association sent questionnaires to librarians or heads of service in 555 colleges across the UK which represented all post-16 educational institutions. A copy of the qustionnaire used in the survey is provided in the Appendices of this report. After two months, a reminder letter was sent to colleges which had not responded.

2.3 Whereas in the previous survey, sixth-form colleges were **excluded** from the sample, in the current research they were included; in some cases therefore 'matched' comparisons with earlier data have been provided by removing sixth-form colleges from the analysis.

2.4 Completed questionnaires were analysed by using the survey analysis package SPSS for Windows.

Reliability of Data and Follow-up Procedures

2.5 As well as asking librarians or heads of service to give detailed information about all library resourcing areas, respondents were also required to provide data about college budgets, total FTE staff and student numbers. Without this information, library-specific data is of limited value. When the survey was conducted in 1992, these college questions produced low-item response rates. In order to address this in the current research, respondents who were unable to provide this information were asked to suggest someone else in the institution who would be able to do so.

4

The listed staff were then contacted by letter with a form to complete and a pre-paid envelope to return the data to the SSRC. Some of those who did not respond were then followed up by telephone.

2.6   A number of other checks were also made. Logic checks and range checks were applied to all questionnaires. Where inconsistencies or contradictory data appeared on questionnaires, respondents were followed-up by telephone for clarification. In some cases, respondents who had omitted to complete certain questions were also followed-up.

Item-response

2.7   As suggested, certain areas within the 1992 survey received a low item response. Where this occurs, the sample upon which inferences can be made and thus the reliability of the data is reduced. In the current research, item-response was generally higher. This was in part owing to the checking process described above; in addition the questionnaire this year allowed respondents to indicate - through the INR (**information not recorded**) box - where their library did not have a system to record the information that was required. Information about levels of INR response is provided in the Appendices.

Survey Response Rate

2.8   Three hundred and eighty-five completed questionnaires were returned to the SSRC; this number included 4 colleges which did not have a library. The overall response rate was therefore 69%. This compares well to the response rate from previous FE college library surveys and to other postal surveys in general.

Response Rates from Previous FE College Library Surveys

2.9   The following table shows the response rate to the survey and provides comparisons with two earlier studies.

Table 2.9   Response Rates to College Library Surveys

	1989	1991-2	Current
Questionnaire sent out	750	485	555
Effective responses	387	264	385
Response rate	52%	54%	69%

3. PROFILE OF COLLEGES

3.1 This section presents information about different aspects of the structure of responding colleges and covers:

- Type of college
- College structure
- Size of college
- Number of sites
- Experience of merger
- Involvement in strategic planning and service delivery initiatives.

3.2 Where appropriate, comparison is made with the previous survey (1991-2). Where comparisons are drawn, interpretation should be made with some caution. Although sixth-form colleges (which were not included in the previous study) can be removed for the purpose of comparisons, other characteristics of the previous sample are not always known.

Type of College

3.3 Colleges were asked to categorise themselves according to the FEFC classification: General Further Education, Sixth-form, Tertiary, Agricultural and Horticultural, Arts and Design and Performing Arts and Designated colleges. As Figure 3.3 illustrates, over half of the responding colleges were general Further Education Colleges (55%). Agriculture and Horticulture, Art and Design and Designated colleges are included in the 'other' category. This category also includes fourteen colleges who indicated that they belonged to two or more of these college types.

Figure 3.3   College Type

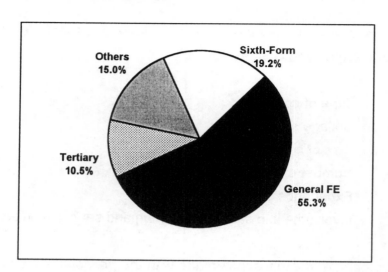

3.4   As suggested in section 3.2, comparison with the previous survey can be made by removing sixth-form colleges from the analysis. This showed that the proportion of General FE Colleges included in this survey was slightly lower than in the earlier research (81% compared with 89% in 1991-2).

3.5   Analysis was conducted to explore whether a relationship existed between type of college and student FTE numbers; results in the form of means and medians are shown in the table below.

Table 3.5   Mean and Median Student FTE Numbers by College Type

College type	Mean	Median	Sample
Sixth Form	899	850	55
General FE	2940	2624	182
Tertiary	2862	2221	35
Other	916	510	47
All Colleges	**2283**	**1832**	**319**

Clear differences emerge here, with general FE colleges having the highest numbers of FTE students.

Position of Library Within College Structure

3.6   Almost half of the colleges who responded (46%) described their library as an autonomous department with a further third indicating that the library was part of a Learning Resources Department (33%).

Figure 3.6   Position of Library within College

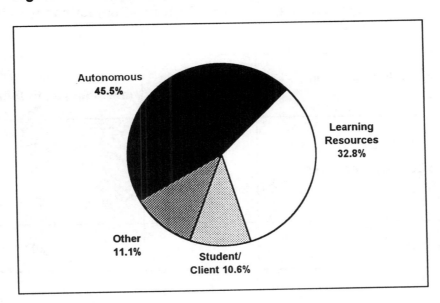

3.7   This element of analysis revealed some key differences.

• Sixth-form colleges were more likely to describe the library as an autonomous unit (69% describing in this way, compared with 19% who said that the library was part of a Learning Resources Department). In other types of college, the proportions identifying the library as autonomous were similar to those who described it as part of Learning Resources Departments.

• Analysis revealed that colleges where libraries were integrated into wider departments were likely to be larger. The mean and median student FTEs of colleges whose libraries were autonomous were 1,876 and 1,370. The comparable figures for colleges where libraries were part of Learning Resources Departments were 2,664 and 2,335. For colleges whose libraries were part of Student/Client services, the mean and median figures were 2,805 and 2,346.

Convergence

3.8   Comparison with the previous survey reveals a shift in the position of the library within the college. In 1991-2 libraries were more likely to be autonomous units. In the table below, sixth-form colleges have been removed from the current data to provide a more accurate comparison with the earlier study.

Table 3.8   Position of Library within College - Comparison with Previous Survey

Position of library within college	1991 - 92 %	1993 - 4 (excluding sixth-form colleges) %
Autonomous	54	40
Part of Learning Resources	24	36
Other	21	24
Sample size	**268**	**307**

College Size

3.9   Numbers of student FTEs are likely to be the most accurate measure of college size. This sample suggests that colleges can be divided into small, medium and large using the following criteria (Table 3.9).

Table 3.9   College Size - Numbers of Students FTE's

Student FTE	Number of Colleges	%
< 1000 (small)	97	30
1000 < 2,500 (medium)	106	33
2,500 + (large)	117	37
Sample size	**320**	**100**

3.10   Investigation of factors affecting college size revealed various statistically significant relationships between structure and types of colleges.

- The large majority both of 'other' colleges and of sixth-form colleges were small (88% and 71% respectively). There were no large sixth-form colleges.

- As suggested in 3.7, larger proportions of institutions where libraries were autonomous were small colleges.

Library Sites

3.11   As Figure 3.11 illustrates, a half of responding libraries had one site. Almost two-thirds of colleges (63%) had just one staffed library site (Table 3.11).

Figure 3.11 Number of College Sites

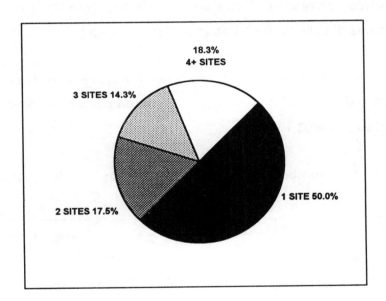

Table 3.11   Number of Sites and Staffed Library Sites

No of sites	% of colleges	% of colleges with indicated no. of Staffed Library sites
1	50	63
2	18	24
3	14	7
4+	18	13
Sample size	**378**	**366**

3.12   All of the sixth-form colleges responding to the survey had just one site (and thus one staffed library site). Generally FE colleges were likely to have more sites than other types of college (69% had more than one site).

3.13   Not surprisingly, larger colleges were likely to have more sites. Ninety-five percent of small colleges had only one site. Eighteen percent of large colleges had four or more sites (Table 3.13).

Table 3.13   Numbers of Staffed Library Sites by College Size

No of sites	%		
	Small	**Medium**	**Large**
1	94	67	34
2	5	25	35
3	1	8	14
4 or more	0	0	17
Sample size	**88**	**104**	**115**

Merger Experience

3.14   Colleges were asked whether they had been involved in a merger in the previous two years and also if they were likely to be involved in a merger within the next year. As Table 3.14 shows, the large majority of colleges responded negatively to both of these questions. Two colleges reported both past and future mergers.

Table 3.14   Past and Future Mergers

Merger experience	No of Colleges	%
Past (two years)	28	7
Future (one year)	12	3
Neither	334	96
Both	2	0
Minimum sample size	**359**	**100**

3.15   Again, there are some notable differences between types of colleges.

- General Further Education colleges were more likely than other types of college to have been affected by a merger (54% of the twenty eight institutions who had experienced a merger were general FE colleges).

- There is some indication, not surprisingly, that those colleges which are anticipating a merger are smaller colleges. The median number of students for colleges anticipating a merger was 979 FTEs, compared with 2500 FTEs for colleges which have been merged and 1920 FTEs for colleges which report neither a past or future merger.

3.16   The picture has changed slightly since 1991-2. At that point, similar proportions reported that they had been affected by a merger (7%) but a larger percentage of colleges were expecting a merger in the next year (10%).

Strategic Planning and Service Delivery Initiatives

3.17 Questions were asked in the current survey to establish the involvement of libraries in aspects of strategic planning and service delivery initiatives. The table below shows that four-fifths of libraries had developed or were in the process of developing a statement of aims and objectives or a strategic plan. The proportions of libraries which had produced - or were producing - a users' charter or service level agreement were much lower (38%).

Table 3.17   Involvement in Strategic Planning and Service Delivery Initiatives

Production of item	% Libraries with statement of aims/objectives or strategic plan	% Libraries with users' charter or service level agreement
Yes	56	18
In preparation	24	20
No	20	62
Sample size	379	379

3.18 Some key differences are suggested below.

- Analysis by type of college revealed that colleges within the 'other' category (that is, agricultural and horticultural, art and design and designated) were less likely to have produced a strategic plan or statement of aims and objectives (32% of these colleges had not been involved in this aspect of strategic planning, where as the figures for the other types of college who responded in this way was approximately 17%).

- Libraries which were part of wider departments (Learning Resources, Student/Client Services or other departments) were more likely to be involved in producing user charters or service level agreements than those which were autonomous units. Analysis conducted on this relationship showed a high level of statistical significance.

- Libraries which had produced or were producing either or both of these items were likely to belong to larger colleges. Table 3.18 shows the figures for the mean and median student FTEs in colleges where this was the case.

Table 3.18   Involvement In Strategic Planning/Service Delivery Initiatives - Means and Medians of Student FTEs

Involvement in initiative	Mean	Median	Sample size
Produced/producing one or both items	2414	2033	259
Produced/producing neither item	1635	1241	60

4. ASPECTS OF PROVISION

4.1 This section presents information from the survey on various aspects of library provision, including:

- Floor area occupied by library services in colleges.
- Reader places available.
- Book stock.
- Levels of automation of services.
- Library opening hours.

Floor Space

4.2 In total, 269 colleges (approximately 70%) were able to provide details on the floor area their library services occupied across all sites. The median floor area occupied by library services was 300, although this figures hides a somewhat skewed distribution. The majority of library services occupied less than 500 square metres in floor space.

Figure 4.2   Floor Area(sq m) Occupied by Library Services (All Sites)

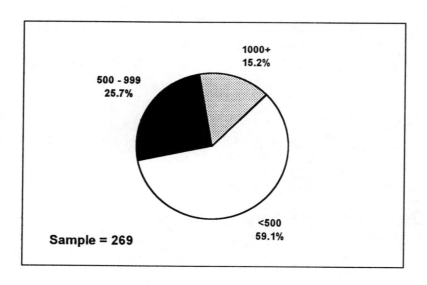

4.3 As expected, the survey results showed a close correlation between library floor space occupied and size of college (number of FTE students). The results indicate a tendency for large colleges to occupy a greater floor area but the pattern is not always consistent. For example, the survey highlights 5 colleges with 2,500+ FTE students (5% of this group) whose library services occupied floor areas of less than 250 square metres. This is clearly outside of the guidelines recommended by the Library Association. This data and other comparisons with the LA Guidelines are included in the Appendices.

Table 4.3   Floor Area Occupied by Size of College

Floor area (Sq.m)	FTE Students		
	Small	Medium	Large
< 250	54	15	5
250 - 499	42	55	16
500 - 999	4	27	42
1000+	0	4	37
Sample size	**69**	**75**	**95**

4.4 The median library services floor area per student FTE was 0.2 square metres.

4.5 The results of the survey also show a significant difference between the library services floor area and both type of college and position of the library within the college. For example

- 94% of sixth-form colleges had floor areas of less than 500 square metres, this being the case for only 47% of general FE colleges. The library floor area per student FTE for these types of colleges were 0.21 square metres for sixth-form colleges and 0.19 square metres for general FE.

- Those libraries which were autonomous departments within the college structure had a tendency to occupy smaller areas of floor space - 68% of libraries which were autonomous departments had floor areas of less than 500 square metres, this being the case for 54% of libraries who were part of learning resources departments.

Reader Places

4.6 The majority of colleges responding to the survey had between 50 and 149 reader places available.

Table 4.6   Number of Reader Places

No.of Places	% of Colleges
< 50	17
50 - 99	29
100 - 149	28
150 +	25
Sample size	374

4.7 The median number of reader places in colleges was 100, this figure showing an increase from the 1991-2 survey result of 91.

4.8 In general, colleges with more FTE students and general Further Education Colleges were more likely to record more reader places. More interestingly, however, is the analysis of reader places per FTE student. Whilst the median number of FTEs per reader place was 16.9, there is considerable variation by type of college.

Table 4.8   Median Number of FTEs per Reader Place by College Type

Type of College	Median No of FTEs per Reader Place per
Sixth form	9.8
General FE	21.7
All Colleges	16.9

Other Aspects of Provision

4.9   The survey also collected information on other aspects of provision, in particular the number of facilities available for use within the library. Only a small proportion (5%) indicated that they had no photocopiers available for student use and similarly, only 6% had no PCs with CD-ROM facilities.

Table 4.9   Library Facilities

Facility	% of Colleges			Sample size
	None	1-2	3+	
Video playback facilities	11	58	31	377
Audio tape recorders	26	34	40	371
Slide projectors	58	32	10	364
Photocopiers for student use	5	82	13	379
PC s with CD-ROM for student use	6	48	46	377
Other PC s for student use	24	18	58	375

Automation

4.10   The survey also sought information on the functions of the college library service which were automated as of 31 July 1994. In particular, respondents were asked to indicate where at least a significant part of the functions were automated at one or more sites. The results (Table 4.10) show approximately two-thirds of colleges

(68%) have automated cataloguing, but that proportionately fewer have extended automation to related functions such as reservations.

Table 4.10   Functions of Library Service which were Automated at 31 July 1994

Function	% of Colleges
Acquisitions	33
Cataloguing	68
Circulation	60
Short Loans	43
Public Access Catalogue	57
Reservations	55
Serials Control	10
Inter-library Loans	6
Access to Information Sources	13
Management Information	30
Other Functions	6
Sample Size	**381**

4.11 Interestingly, in a quarter of colleges (26%), none of the library functions were automated.

4.12 For most functions, the general Further Education colleges were more likely to be automated than other types of college (Table 4.12). The notable exceptions to this were in the functions of short loans, management information and (to a lesser extent) circulation, where sixth-form colleges were more commonly automated than FE colleges.

Table 4.12   Automated Functions by Type of College

Function	% of Colleges			
	Sixth Form	General FE	Tertiary	Other
Acquisitions	29	37	33	25
Cataloguing	67	71	65	58
Circulation	66	64	60	40
Short Loans	53	44	42	26
Public Access Catalogue	53	61	55	49
Reservations	60	60	52	33
Serials Control	5	12	8	9
Inter - library Loans	3	7	5	5
Access to Information Sources	7	18	12	7
Management Information	36	30	38	18
Other Functions	6	6	5	4
Sample Size	**73**	**210**	**40**	**57**

4.13   Overall, only 21% of general FE colleges had no functions automated, this being the case for 25% of sixth-form, 32% of tertiary and 37% of other types of college.

4.14   In addition to college type, levels of automation might also be expected to be correlated (independently) with size of college. This is borne out by the survey - those with **no functions automated** being as follows:

- 32% of colleges with less than 1,000 FTE students
- 25% of colleges with between 1,000 and 2,499 FTE students
- 15% of colleges with 2,500 + FTE students

4.15 Generally, automated library functions appear to be more common in colleges where the library service is part of a Learning Resource Department. Where this was the case, only 20% of such colleges had no automated functions; the comparable figures for libraries which were autonomous units and those in Student/Client Services were 28% and 35% respectively.

Bookstock

4.16 The total bookstock and number of periodicals taken by college libraries which responded to the survey are shown in Tables 4.16a and 4.16b, together with comparable data from the 1991-2 survey.

Table 4.16a   Library Bookstock

Number of Books	% of Colleges	
	1991/92	1993/94
<10,000	16	18
10,000 - 19,999	24	24
20,000 - 29,999	26	30
30,000 - 39,999	14	10
40,000 +	19	18
Sample size	257	347

Table 4.16b   Number of Periodicals taken

Number of Periodicals	% of Colleges	
	1991/92	1993/94
<50	16	19
50 - 99	24	21
100 - 149	26	21
150 - 199	14	14
200 - 249	12	9
250 +	18	16
Sample size	355	100

4.17 For Table 4.16a, the comparison of the 1991-2 bookstock position and that of 1993-4 reveals close similarities, the key difference being the proportionately few colleges recording high (30,000+) bookstock in 1993-4. This figure is borne out by further analysis. Bookstock for colleges included in the surveys appears to have declined between 1992 and 1995. The median bookstock for each of the years was

- 22,000 in 1991-2
- 20,000 in 1993-4

4.18 Additional analysis, however, suggests that this difference is due to the more comprehensive coverage of this (1993-4) survey. In addition to a higher rate of response, the current survey also included sixth-form colleges, which, as might have been expected, tend to have a smaller bookstock than other types of college. Table 4.19 provides details of the median bookstock by type of college - sixth-form colleges have an average bookstock of only 9,409, compared with 22,186 for general FE colleges.

Table 4.18   Median Stock Figures by Type of College

Stock Type	Median Stock				
	Sixth Form	General FE	Tertiary	Other	All Colleges
Books	9409	22186	20165	12000	20,000
Periodical titles	35	152	130	108	120
CD-ROMs	11	12	10	8	10
Films/Videotapes	80	252	256	200	222
Audio tapes	43	79	25	12	60

4.19 Examining other aspects of library stock again suggests that general FE colleges have higher median stock levels than other types of college. Table 4.18 provides details.

4.20   A factor of key importance in assessing library resources is the number of books per FTE student in colleges. Overall, the median figure for books per student FTE was 11.03, the comparable figures for different types of college being presented in Table 4.20. Clear differences are evident, with the median for sixth-form colleges being higher than for other types of college.

Table 4.20   Median Books per FTE Student by College Type

Type of College	Median Books per FTE
Sixth Form	12.56
General FE	10.25
Tertiary	11.15
Other	17.26
All Colleges	**11.03**

Further analysis suggests that there is a link between college size and bookstock. Figure 4.20 below highlights this - the figure has been produced for the main body of the data with outliers removed.

Figure 4.20   Books per FTE student by College Size

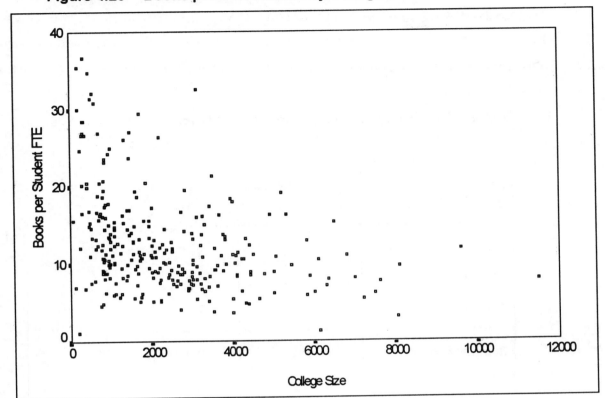

4.21   As in the 1991-2 survey, over half of the colleges included in the 1993-4 research had total additions to bookstock in the year of less than 1,500 books.

Table 4.21   Additions to Bookstock

Books added	% of Colleges	
	1991-2	1993-4
< 500	10	14
500- 999	23	22
1000- 1499	22	18
1500- 1999	14	12
2000 - 2499	14	10
2500+	18	23
Sample size	**222**	**275**

4.22   The median number of additions to bookstock for the two surveys are very similar - 1,310 for the 1991-2 year and 1,311 for 1993-4.

4.23   Table 4.23 shows the replenishment rate of the bookstock in colleges.

Table 4.23   Replenishment Rate of Bookstock

Replenishment Rate of Bookstock	No of colleges	%
< 5%	83	31
5% - 10%	110	41
10% +	74	28
Sample size	267	100

4.24   Respondents were also asked to report on how many withdrawals from their bookstock they had made. The findings are presented below.

Table 4.24   Withdrawals from Bookstock

No of Withdrawals	No of Colleges	%
< 250	63	29
250 < 750	51	23
750 < 1500	41	19
1500 +	62	29
Sample size	217	100

Levels of Activity

4.25   The total number of opening hours per week in responding colleges ranged from 12 to 334 in term-time, and from 0 to 196.5 during vacations. The median number of opening hours per week was 53 in term-time and 35 during vacations.   These medians do not differ greatly from results from in 1991-2 (where the comparable figures were 52 and 37).   Tables 4.25a and 4.25b illustrate the range and distribution of opening hours across colleges in term-time and vacations.

Table 4.25a   Weekly Term-time Opening Hours (All Sites)

Term-time Opening Hours	No of Colleges	%
< 45	97	26
45 < 90	175	46
90 < 135	65	17
135 +	41	11
Sample size	378	100

Table 4.25b   Vacation Opening Hours (All Sites)

Vacation Opening Hours	No of Colleges	%
< 20	99	28
20 < 40	135	37
40 < 60	68	19
60 +	58	16
Sample size	360	100

4.26   When analysis of term-time opening hours was examined further by student FTE, the following observations were made:

- The library was open for longer per student FTE in sixth-form and 'other' colleges.

- In small colleges, libraries were open for more hours per student FTE. In 76% of small colleges, the figure was one twentieth of an hour per FTE; this was the case for 6% of large colleges.

Care is needed in interpreting these results given the obvious limitations on available opening hours in a week.

Visits

4.27   Tables 4.27a and 4.27b examine the term-time and vacation visits. It should be noted that the item-response to this question is low, with around a half of respondents not reporting about visits (see Appendices for discussion about levels of INR - information not recorded).

Table 4.27a   Weekly Term-Time Visits

Visits per week	No of Colleges	%
< 1400	56	30
1400 - < 3000	52	28
3000 +	79	42
Sample size	**187**	**100**

Table 4.27b   Weekly Vacation Visits

Visits per week	No of Colleges	%
< 20	75	44
20 - < 100	31	18
100 +	65	38
Sample size	171	100

4.28   Comparison with the 1991-2 survey indicates key differences - strikingly higher proportions of colleges reported more than 3,000 visits per week in the current study (42% compared with a much smaller figure, 13%, in 1991-2).

4.29   Unravelling the reasons for this may be complex. As has been suggested earlier, comparison of the two datasets is difficult because some characteristics of the previous sample are not known.

4.30   However, inferences based on information that the data can provide and on knowledge of changes in the FE sector may assist understanding of these results. Analysis reveals the following:

- Large colleges were more likely to provide information about visits than small colleges (58% of large colleges did so compared with 54% of medium and 37% of small colleges).

- Types of **predominantly small** colleges (sixth-form and 'other') were correspondingly less likely to report about visits.

- It may be assumed that smaller colleges are less likely to have gate count facilities in their libraries.

4.31   It might be argued that these factors will have applied - possibly even more so - when the previous survey was undertaken. However, other changes may also be critical. In particular, it is known that student numbers in colleges have grown. Comparison of the two surveys confirms this. In 1991-2, 25% of colleges responding reported over 3,000 student FTEs; the corresponding percentage in 1993-4 is 37%. The contrast is in fact more stark as a sizeable proportion of sixth-form colleges are included in the current study and these are known to be smaller colleges.

4.32   Not surprisingly, analysis by college size indicates that larger colleges receive more weekly visits. Differences also occur by college type.

Table 4.32   Term-time Weekly Visits by College Type

Weekly visits	%		
	Sixth Form	General FE	Tertiary
< 1400	56	27	18
1400 - > 3000	33	36	19
3000 +	10	37	63

4.33   However, when the numbers of weekly visits are examined per student FTE a slightly different picture emerges. Small colleges are likely to receive more visits per FTE though differences are not statistically significant. Comparisons cannot be made with the previous survey here as comparable data from that research is not available.

4.34 Table 4.34 shows the profile of issue transactions recorded by libraries. Sixty-one percent of libraries recorded fewer than 500 issues per week. The median number of issues was 350.

Table 4.34   Issues Per Week

Weekly Issues	No of Colleges	%
< 250	102	34
250 < 500	81	27
500 < 750	58	19
750 +	59	20
Sample size	300	101

4.35 Comparison with the earlier survey is provided below, with sixth-form colleges again removed.

Table 4.35   Comparison of 1991-2/1993-4 Surveys: Weekly Issues

| Weekly Issues | % | |
	1991-2	1993-4
< 250	26	24
250 < 500	25	30
500 < 750	23	22
750 +	27	24
Median Issues	491	445
Sample size	230	245

4.36   It may be surprising that results for issues transactions are similar or lower than those seen in 1991-92, when other indicators of activity levels, in particular, visits, have risen so dramatically.   Analysis of issue transactions per FTE for the two surveys would be an efficient means of comparison but unfortunately data of this kind is not available for the earlier research.

4.37   Possible explanations for this might include the lack of availability of core texts (since student numbers have risen to such a degree).   The shift towards electronic information in many colleges might also contribute to this situation.   Analysis to determine whether there was a relationship between CD-ROM expenditure and levels of issues suggested that this was the case, although consideration of other factors may be necessary.

4.38   Analysis of the relationship between issue transactions and college size suggests, not surprisingly, that larger colleges issue more items.   However, when issues per FTE by college size is analysed, the picture is again somewhat different with smaller colleges dealing with larger number of issues.   The relationship between college size and issues per student FTE is statistically significant.

Table 4.38   Weekly Issues per Student FTE: College Size

Weekly Issues per student FTE	%		
	Small	Medium	Large
< 0.15	25	21	34
0.15 < 0.3	32	48	46
0.3+	43	31	20

4.39   Clearly the relationship between library staff-student ratio and levels of activity in different colleges requires extensive investigation.

Additional Issues

4.40 Various comments about different aspects of provision were provided by respondents to the survey. As suggested earlier, some respondents indicated that it was very difficult or not possible to isolate library-specific facilities in a wider Learning Resources Department. Some colleges, particularly those which were small, had few facilities of particular types within the library (for example, PCs, photocopiers) and suggested that some of these items were available in the college generally. In some cases, such items were located in other parts of the college, for example in IT departments.

5.   FINANCE

5.1   This section reviews the survey findings in the following areas:

- Expenditure on salaries and non-salary categories
- Relationship of library and college budgets
- Stock replenishment rates

Financial Year

5.2   As table 5.2 illustrates, for 83% of responding colleges, 1993-4 was a 16-month financial year. For the purposes of this research, all figures were standardised to a 12-month period. Inconsistencies within some questionnaires suggest that a small number of colleges may have indicated that figures were provided for one period where they had in fact supplied them for the other. Therefore some caution in interpretation is advised.

Table 5.2   Financial Year Adhered To

Financial Year	No of Colleges	%
16 month	311	83
12 month	63	17
Sample size	**374**	**100**

5.3   Decisions about the size of the library budget were likely to be made by the Principal or College Director (29%), a Vice, Assistant or Deputy Principal (27%), a Finance Director or other college finance officer (11%) or a combination of college managers (11%). Six percent of colleges responding indicated that their Librarian or Head of Service made this decision. Further information about the role of the Librarian or Head of Service can be seen in Section 6.

Library Budget

5.4 Survey respondents were asked to detail their library expenditure excluding salaries. Approximately half of the libraries had expenditure of under £20,000, the median expenditure being £26,411. This compares with a median expenditure recorded in the 1991-2 survey of £19,850.

Table 5.4   Total Library Budget (Excluding Salaries)

Expenditure	No of Colleges	%
< 10,000	70	20
10,000 < 20,000	98	27
20,000 < 40,000	108	30
40,000 +	82	23
Sample size	**358**	**100**

5.5 The non-salaries expenditure of almost all sixth-form colleges responding was less than £20,000. Six percent of sixth-form colleges had non-salaries budgets of more than this amount, compared with 73% of general FE colleges. The relationship between type of college and non-salaries library expenditure shows a high level of significance.

5.6   The following table summarises college expenditure on library staff salaries for 1993-4.

Table 5.6   Library Expenditure (Including Salaries)

Expenditure (£)	No of Colleges	%
< 40,000	71	31
40,000 < 80,000	64	28
80,000 < 120,000	38	16
120,000 +	57	25
Sample size	230	100

5.7   The survey results demonstrate some significant differences between expenditure and some aspects of colleges. For example

- As expected, sixth-form colleges (which were mainly smaller) had lower budgets - none of these colleges had a total budget exceeding £80,000. General FE colleges were likely to spend more than this amount (63% did so). The corresponding figures for tertiary and other colleges spending more than £80,000 were 42% and 19%.

- Again, it was not surprising that budgets for large colleges tended to be larger. Perhaps more surprisingly, results show that the budgets of two small colleges exceeded £120,000 while three large colleges spent less than £40,000.

Expenditure on Resources

5.8   Tables 5.8a, b and c show levels of expenditure on books, periodicals and CD-ROMs.

Table 5.8a   Expenditure on Books

Expenditure (£)	No of Colleges	%
< 5,000	53	18
5,000 - 10,000	78	26
10,000 - 15,000	59	20
15,000 - 20,000	40	13
20,000+	69	23
Sample size	299	100

Table 5.8b   Expenditure on Periodicals

Expenditure (£)	No of Colleges	%
< 2,500	104	35
2,500 - 5,000	64	22
5,000 - 7,500	43	14
7,500 - 10,000	36	12
10,000+	49	17
Sample size	296	100

Table 5.8c **Expenditure on CD-ROMs**

Expenditure (£)	No of Colleges	%
< 1,000	82	55
1,000 - < 2,000	52	20
2,000+	67	25
Sample size	**267**	**100**

Ratio of Library to College Budget

5.9 The ratio of library to college budget was less than 1% for approximately half of responding colleges (52%). Mean and median values were 1.5% and 1% respectively.

Table 5.9 **Ratio of Library to College Budget**

Ratio (%)	No of Colleges	%
< 0.5%	71	31
0 5% < 1%	60	21
1 < 1.5%	69	25
1.5% +	64	23
Sample size	**279**	**100**

5.10 The following significant differences were observed.

- Libraries within 66% of sixth-form colleges received less than 1% of the college budget. Those libraries in tertiary and 'other' colleges were likely to receive more than 1%. This analysis revealed highly significant differences.

- Libraries situated in Student/Client Services were likely to receive a smaller proportion of the college budget than their counterparts in other structures. The budget of a large majority of these libraries (78%) was less than 1% of the total college budget; this was the case for 50% of both libraries which were autonomous and those which were within Learning Resources Departments. Means and medians for this analysis are shown below.

Table 5.10   Ratio of Library to College Budget: Position of Library

Position of library	Mean	Median
Autonomous departments	1.44%	1.18%
Learning Resources Department	1.46%	1.29%
Student/Client Services Department	1.07%	0.98%
Other	1.95%	1.29%

Library Expenditure per FTE

5.11 Table 5.11 shows that just under half of the responding colleges spent less than £15.00 per student in 1993-4. It also illustrates that a quarter of colleges spent £25 or more. The mean and median values were £21 and £16.66 respectively.

Figure 5.11   Library Expenditure (Excluding Salaries) by Student FTE

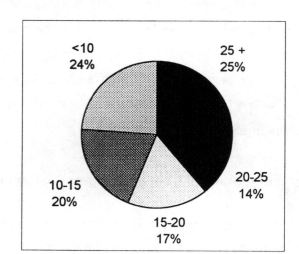

5.12   Further analysis conducted to determine whether other factors were related to levels of expenditure revealed significant differences between types of college.

5.13   Sixth-form colleges were likely to spend less per student (63% spent less than the median amount for all colleges, £16.74).   The majority of 'other' colleges (66%) spent more than £25.00 per student FTE. Means and medians for different college types are presented below.

Table 5.13   Library Expenditure per Student FTE by College Type - Means and Medians

Type of College	Mean £	Median £
Sixth - form	14.85	11.02
FE	18.24	16.67
Tertiary	20.23	14.90
Other	43.45	34.95

5.14 Small colleges were likely to spend more per student FTE than their medium or large counterparts. Tables 5.14a and 5.14b below suggest a relationship between non-salaries expenditure and college size which is highly significant. Table 5.14a illustrates how much small, medium and large colleges spent on students; Table 5.14b shows the means and medians for this analysis.

Table 5.14a Expenditure per Student FTE: College Size

£	College size (%)		
	Small	Medium	Large
< 10	21	23	26
10 - 15	8	25	25
15 - 20	12	17	20
20 - 25	11	19	12
25 +	47	15	17

Table 5.14b Expenditure per Student FTE by College Size - Means and Medians

College size	Mean	Median
Small (< 1000)	30.96	24.04
Medium (1000 - < 2,500)	17.58	15.84
Large (2,500+)	17.73	14.84

5.15 A comparison of expenditure per student FTE can be made here with the 1991-2 data although caution is required due to the limited reliability of the earlier survey data. The results show a median expenditure per student FTE of £9.60 in 1991-2, compared with £14.84 in 1993-4.

Budget Increases 1993-4/1994-5

5.16   Findings from analysis of library budget changes from 1993-4/1994-5 are presented below. In most cases, it is not possible to attribute differences to particular factors as the survey focus was on 1993-4 only. Some calculations are based on low sample sizes: this has occurred when respondents were not able to supply both sets of required data. As the table indicates, 20% of those colleges included in this analysis (70 colleges) indicated that their 1994-5 non-salaries budget was smaller than that for 1993-4.

Figure 5.16a   Library Budget Increase (Excluding Salaries) 1993-4/1994-5

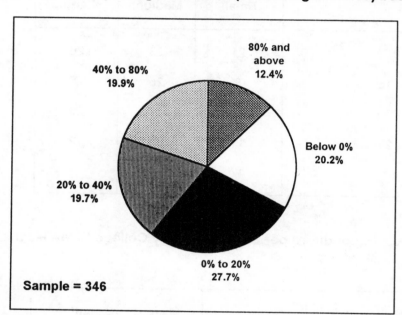

Table 5.16b   Library Budget Increase (including salaries) 1993-4/1994-5

% Increase	No of Colleges	%
< 0	26	12
0 < 20	64	30
20 < 40	69	32
40 < 80	54	25
Sample Size	**213**	**99**

5.17   Budget increases for particular stock items - books, periodicals, and CD-ROMs were also analysed.   Figures 5.17a, b and c illustrate these budget changes (tables providing this information can be seen in the Appendices)

Figure 5.17a   Book Budget Increase

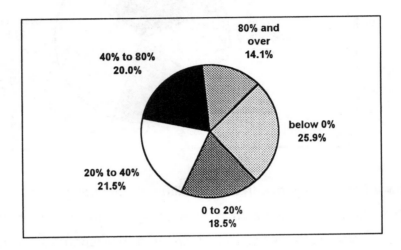

Figure 5.17b   Periodicals Budget Increase

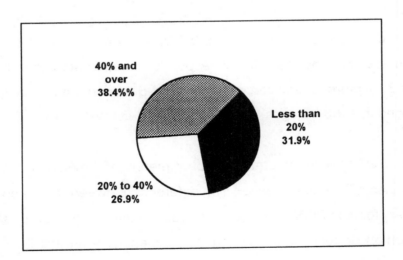

Figure 5.17c CD-ROMs Budget Increase

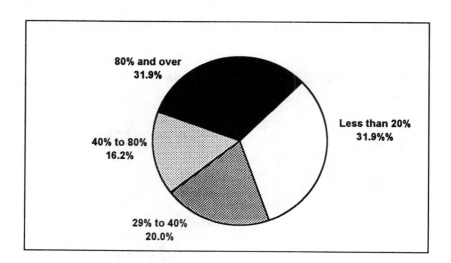

5.18   There was some evidence that expenditure on periodicals had increased at a higher rate in sixth-form colleges than in other college types. Small colleges (many of them sixth-form) also appeared to have increased their spending on this stock item at a greater rate than their medium or large counterparts; the differences by size of college were statistically significant.

5.19   Evidence about expenditure on CD-ROMs is perhaps more interesting. As Table 5.17c shows, almost a third of respondents anticipated that they would spend at least 80% more on this stock item in 1994-5 than in the previous year. A quarter of respondents (53 colleges) intended to spend at least 100% more on CD-ROMs.

5.20   Table 5.20 provides information about means and medians of budget increases in stock items described above. The difference between the mean and median in the figures for CD-ROMs budget changes reinforces the suggestion above that a proportion of colleges increasing their expenditure on this item had done so by a substantial amount. The wide distribution of these figures suggested that while many colleges were investing in CD-ROMs in 1994-5, some had done so in the previous academic year.

Table 5.20   Budget Increases in Stock Items - Means and Medians

% Increase	%	
	Mean	Median
Books	39	24
Periodicals	35	33
CD-ROMs	111	33

6. STAFFING

6.1 In this section the following areas are considered:

- Status of librarian or head of service
- Professional and library support staff
- Library staff per student FTE

6.2 A large part of this section is based on responses to three questions. One of these questions asked respondents how many FTE staff they had in different categories; the other two required more detailed information about the numbers, grades and gender of staff in professionally qualified or management posts and for those in library support posts. In some cases, answers provided for these two different sets of questions did not match and therefore some caution in interpretation should be advised.

Status of Librarian

6.3 Aspects relating to the status of the Librarian or Head of Service were explored in different questions.

6.4 Respondents were not asked directly if the staff member in direct operational control of the library was a chartered librarian. As a proxy, those who held both a degree or higher level qualification in library or information studies and were members of the Library Association were identified. Forty-eight percent of staff who were in direct operational control of the library fell into this category.

6.5 A question was asked to establish the relationship of the Librarian or Head of Service with the Senior Management Team. As Table 6.5 indicates, only a small proportion (4%) were members in their own right and the large majority (78%) reported directly to a Senior Management Team (SMT) member.

Table 6.5   **Relationship of Librarian/Head of Service with Senior Management Team**

Relationship	No of Colleges	%
Member in own right	15	4
Reports directly to SMT member	294	78
Reports indirectly to SMT via someone else	60	16
Other	9	2
Sample size	**378**	**100**

6.6   The median number of student FTEs in those small sample of colleges which said that their Head of Service was a member of the Senior Management Team was 2,400; the corresponding figure for colleges who said their Head of Service reported directly to an SMT member was 1,800 FTEs and it was 1930 for those who reported indirectly to the SMT. Analysis of this question by size of college did not reveal any significant differences.

6.7   As indicated earlier, a small percentage of colleges (6%) said that their Librarian or Head of Service decided the size of the total library budget.

6.8   Respondents were asked how much input the Librarian or Head of Service had into the decision about the library budget. The results can be seen in Table 6.8.

Table 6.8   Input of Librarian/Head of Service into Decision About Size of Budget

Level of input	No of Colleges	%
A great deal	82	22
Some	138	37
Very little	77	20
None at all	78	21
Sample size	**375**	**100**

6.9   While, overall, in 59% of colleges, the Librarian or Head of Service had a great deal or some input into decisions about the size of the library budget (Table 6.8), this was the case for 81% of colleges where the Librarian or Head of Service was a member of the SMT.

6.10   Table 6.10 shows the grades and gender of the person in direct operational control of the library for colleges in England, Northern Ireland and Wales.

Table 6.10   Grade and Gender of Person in Charge of Library (England, Northern Ireland and Wales)

Grade	%	%	
		Male	Female
APC3 or less	3	0	100
Sc 4 - 6	30	14	86
SO 1 - 2	22	6	94
PO range	4	29	71
Lecturer	6	21	79
Senior Lecturer	7	39	61
Management Spine	16	42	58
Other	11	31	69
Sample size	**317**	**67**	**249**

6.11   As the table indicates, in a third of colleges, the library was managed by someone of APC grade 6 or below. The results also indicate that male staff managing the library represent 21% (67 from 317 colleges) of library managers (defined here as those in direct operational control). The table further shows that male library managers are more likely to be in more senior grades. For example:

- 37% of female library managers were on APC 6 or below. The corresponding figure for male library managers was 19%.

- 52% of male library managers were at lecturer/senior lecturer or Management Spine level; this was the case for 24% of female library managers.

6.12 Analysis of questionnaires from Scotland was conducted separately as grades across nations were not always equivalent. Male managers represented a third of those in this role. The sample is small - 24 colleges.

Table 6.12   Grade and Gender of Person in Charge of Library (Scotland)

Grade	%	% Male	% Female
APIII - APV	46	9	91
PO	4	100	0
Lecturer/Librarian	4	29	71
Higher Staff	16	42	58
Other	4	0	100
Sample size	**24**	**8**	**16**

6.13 Again, it appears that male library managers are more likely than their female counterparts to be in more senior grades:

- A half of the women who managed libraries were on scale APV or below, this was the case for 13% of men in this role.

- 31% of female library managers were Lecturers/Librarians or Higher staff; the comparable figure for men was 50%.

6.14 Responding colleges were asked to provide figures for FTE library staffing in different categories. Table 6.14a shows the numbers of FTE staff in professionally qualified or management posts within the library while Table 6.14b shows numbers of staff in library support roles.

Figure 6.14a Number of FTE Professionally Qualified/Management Posts (England, Northern Ireland and Wales)

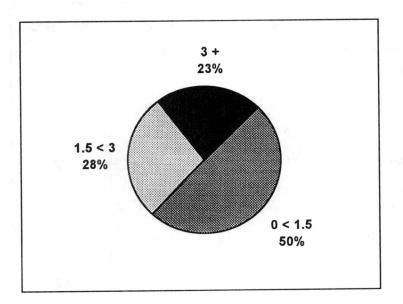

Figure 6.14b Number of FTE Library Support Posts (England, Northern Ireland and Wales)

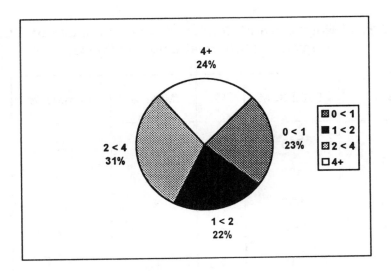

6.15 The number (total and FTE) and gender distribution of these posts were also examined. Tables 6.14a and 6.14b look at professionally qualified and management staff and at library support workers in England, Northern Ireland and Wales.

Table 6.15a   Numbers and Gender Distribution of Professionally Qualified and Management Staff (England, Northern Ireland and Wales)

Grade	Total Staff	%	Male %	Female %	Total FTEs
Sc 4 - 6	404	49	15	85	350.257
SO 1 - 2	144	17	14	86	129.54
PO	29	4	21	79	27.5
Lecturer	72	9	21	79	62.3
Senior Lecturer	29	4	41	59	29
Management Spine	69	8	39	61	67.5
Other	77	9	18	82	64.64
Sample Size	**824**	**100**	**155**	**669**	**730.737**

Table 6.15b   Numbers and Gender Distribution of Library Support Staff (England, Northern Ireland and Wales)

Grade	Total Staff	%	Male %	Female %	Total FTEs
Sc 1	238	16	8	92	140.18
Sc 1 - 2	421	27	7	93	273.62
Sc 2 - 3	662	43	6	94	479.1
Sc 4 - 6	93	6	16	84	77.72
Other	119	8	10	90	74.96
Sample Size	**1,533**	**100**	**114**	**1,419**	**1,045.58**

6.16   The following observations can be made:

- Almost a half of the professionally qualified or management posts (total not FTE) were on scale 4-6 (49%).

- 43% of those in library support posts were on scale 1 or scale 1-2.

6.17   Women represented 79% of the professional and management staff and 93% of library support staff. Although women formed the majority of the workforce, they were less likely to be in senior positions. For example, of male professionals or managers in the library, 8% were senior lecturers and 27% were on the management spine; of women in this section of the workforce, 3% were senior lecturers and 6% were on the management spine.

6.18   Similar analysis for Scottish colleges was also undertaken and findings are presented below.

Table 6.18a   Number and Gender Distribution of Professionally Qualified and Management Staff (Scotland)

Grade	Total Staff	%	Male %	Female %	Total FTEs
AP IV - V	13	28	8	92	13
PO	1	2	100	0	1
Lecturer/Librarian	6	13	33	67	6
Senior Lecturer /Chief Librarian	5	11	40	60	5
Higher Staff	5	11	80	20	5
Other	16	35	6	94	16
Sample size	**46**	**100**	**11**	**35**	**46**

Table 6.18b Number and Gender Distribution of Library Support Staff (Scotland)

Grade	Total Staff	%	Male %	Female %	Total FTEs
Sc 1	6	8	0	100	3.7
Sc 2- 3	37	52	12	88	32.10
API -II	9	13	22	78	8.5
APIII - IV	3	4	33	67	3
Other	16	23	38	62	13.90
Sample size	71	100	13	58	61.2

6.19 A similar link between gender and grade was seen in these results, notably that women exceed men in the workforce but are more likely to occupy the lower grades.

FTE Student : Library Staff

6.20 The ratio of library staff to FTE students is a critical indicator of resourcing levels in college libraries. Mean and median values were 1:496 and 1:433 per student FTE respectively. Further details are provided in Table 6.20, which indicates that only 23% of colleges had ratios of less than 1:300.

Table 6.20   Ratio of FTE Students to FTE Library Staff

FTE Students	No of Colleges	%
< 300	75	23
300 < 400	59	19
400 < 500	64	20
500 < 600	48	15
600 +	71	23

Figure 6.20   Ratio of FTE Students to FTE Library Staff

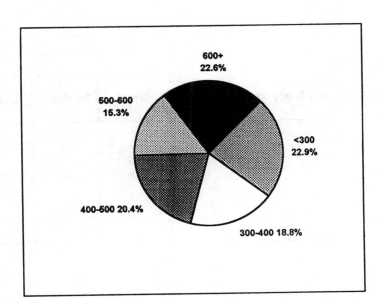

6.21   Further analysis revealed the following highly significant differences:

- Sixth-form colleges were likely to have fewer staff per FTE student (60% of such colleges had more than 500 FTE students per staff member compared to 38% of general FE, 29% of tertiary and 16% of other colleges). By contrast, 'other' colleges tended to have a higher library staff:student ratio - 61% had fewer than 300 FTE per library staff member, this being the case for 13% of sixth-form, 16% of general FE and 26% of tertiary colleges.

- Small colleges tended to have a higher staff:student ratio (Table 6.21)

Table 6.21   Ratio of FTE Students to FTE Library Staff by College Size

FTE students per library staff member	College size		
	Small	Medium	Large
< 300	43	17	14
300 < 400	18	22	16
400 < 500	12	22	25

Additional Issues

6.22   This section of the questionnaire gave some indication of the level of changes within FE and within libraries. Some of the questions about staffing presented problems for respondents. In some colleges, the staffing structure of libraries which were part of wider departments had been transformed and traditional library-specific posts were being eroded. In many cases, for example, library support posts were being broadened to incorporate technical aspects for use across Learning Resources Departments. Library technicians were a feature in some colleges. It was clear too that many managers had a remit which far exceeded control of the library; such staff were not necessarily librarians by background and did not therefore have library-specific qualifications. In addition, respondents from several colleges indicated that some qualified librarians occupied library support posts.

7. CONCLUSIONS

7.1 This final section considers some critical issues arising from the survey. These include: an assessment of the strength of the data, consideration of the findings alongside areas highlighted as important to address in the previous survey, and some discussion about how libraries are or are not meeting guidelines for provision suggested by the Library Association (1995).

7.2 Undoubtedly, the 1993-4 survey has provided substantial and sound data about the current picture of provision in FE college libraries. The strength of the data has been established in two ways. *Data reliability* was confirmed by a high overall response to the survey and by ascertaining that responding colleges were reasonably representative by type and across the nations. A high degree of *validity* too was achieved by piloting the questionnaire extensively. The logic, range and other checks applied to completed questionnaires did raise further small concerns about validity; however, most of these could be attributed to the widely differing circumstances of libraries often resulting from the high level of change within the sector. The implications of these changing contexts, for future research, are further explored below.

7.3 The report of the 1991-2 survey, *College Libraries - A Case for Investment* (Bibby, Eastwood and Wisher, 1994) was able to point to particular issues which were clearly playing an increasing part in the debate about library provision. Some of these issues have been addressed in this survey. In particular, the survey looked at the degree to which library services were 'embedded' within college structures, recognising that this might be one key factor in appropriate resourcing and provision. This integration into college structures was examined by investigating the role of libraries in strategic planning, and by looking at other indicators of this integration such as the relationship of the Librarian or Head of Service with the Senior Management Team and their involvement in budgetary decisions. There was much evidence of increasing involvement in certain aspects of strategic planning and other service delivery initiatives - with a majority of colleges reporting library involvement in preparing strategic plans or statements of aims and objectives albeit that much smaller proportions had produced users' charters or service level agreements. However, other aspects of 'embeddedness' or integration into college structures were arguably less positive. For example, very small proportions of Librarians or Heads of Service were involved in Senior Management and large proportions had little or no say in decisions about the library budget. There was evidence in these, as in many other elements of library provision, that college size was one important predictor of the status of the library within the college; libraries in colleges which were larger being more likely to have been involved in strategic planning initiatives and to have greater say in senior management decisions and in budgetary matters.

7.4   Numerous other areas of service provision and development are highlighted by this survey. Perhaps those of key importance are:

- the technological change which is being utilised by library services and the effects of this on, for example, traditional bookstock and expenditure on CD-ROM materials

- the role of library staff within both the rapidly changing library service and the 'converging' of what were previously autonomous departments

- differences in resourcing which may be influenced by the position of the library within the college

- the clear gender bias which exists in the grade profile of library staff in colleges.

Each of these poses both problems and challenges for library services in the future as the library increasingly becomes a 'resource for learning'.

7.5   While the main thrust of this report has been to examine levels of provision and to look at factors which may influence these, another crucial perspective is offered by exploring the data alongside the Library Association guidelines for provision (Library Association, 1995). These guidelines have been developed to 'provide practical advice on what needs to be done to provide a library that meets the needs of students' (Carl Clayton, 1995). The guidelines are deliberately set as a 'target' for colleges seeking to achieve best practice. Not withstanding this, where such analysis has been conducted, a worrying picture emerges as in each case, a large majority of colleges have effectively reported that they were unable to meet the criteria outlined. Clearly there are serious implications of this that should be addressed both by the Library Association and by FE funding bodies.

7.6   Finally, as suggested earlier in this section, one of the difficulties in conducting this survey was matching areas for investigation with libraries which are extremely different from each other; this is a reflection of 'where libraries are' within the developments that have taken place in both libraries themselves and in the FE sector in the last few years. A library which is an autonomous unit may well be resourced and managed quite differently from one which is part of a Learning Resources Department. Indeed many of the latter - and other libraries which were part of converged departments - found it extremely difficult to provide library-specific data largely because finance, resources and even staffing crossed the boundaries of **all** units within the wider department. It is vital that future research is able to address these highly important factors affecting library provision and takes account of the qualitative shift which has occurred and which is occurring in the way that services are delivered.

8. REFERENCES

Beckett, F, Unbalanced Books, *TES Further Education Update*, March 3 1995.

Bibby, J, Eastwood R and Wisher S J (1994), *College Libraries: A Case for Investment?* The Library Association Professional Practice Department,1994.
ISBN 1 872088 066

Clayton, C, (1995), Beyond the Stereotype, *FE Now* (18) June 1995.

Crequer, N, Terms of Empowerment, *Times Higher*, March 17 1995.

FEFC (1994), *Quality and Standards in Further Education in England, Chief Inspector's Annual Report 1993-4*, FEFC: Coventry.

Library Association, (1989), 1989 College and Polytechnic Survey (mimeo., 4 +11pp).

Library Association, (1992), *Statistical Survey of College Libraries* - 1991-2 (mimeo, 8pp).

Library Association, (1995), *Guidelines for College Libraries*, Library Association Publishing,1995.ISBN 185604 153 0

APPENDICES

Survey of College Libraries

The purpose of this survey is to build up a picture of library provision in the academic year 1993-4. It aims to identify what are the areas of good practice in college libraries and where there are further resourcing needs. Such information will build upon previous research, notably the survey conducted by the Library Association in 1991-2 and outlined in *College Libraries - A Case for Investment?*.

The questionnaire is straightforward to complete.

- Mostly you simply need to **tick a box** or to insert information in the space provided.

- **Some** detailed information is requested. You may need to speak to colleagues to obtain this information.

- Please complete one questionnaire for each college but remember that information is required about all sites offering staffed library services.

- Where information requested is not recorded, please indicate this in the appropriate box (labelled INR).

- Mostly, information is requested for the year 1993-4, and many questions use a census date of 31 July 1994. Some questions are asked about the current situation. *Please remember that 1993-4 was a 16-month financial year.*

- In many colleges the library forms part of a converged service along with other services such as computing or reprographics. Our pilot has shown that in almost all cases, it is possible to identify the required figures for the library/resource centre separately from other, non-library aspects. If this is not possible, please provide an explanatory note where relevant. The research team may contact you for clarification.

When you have completed the questionnaire, please return it in the pre-paid envelope provided.

THE ORGANISATION

1   Name of person completing
this questionnaire

....

Telephone number

....

2   Job title of person completing
this questionnaire

....

Fax number or email address

....

3   Name and address of college

....

....

....

Telephone *(if different from above)* ....

4   What kind of college is it?

Sixth-form   ☐

General Further Education   ☐

Agricultural & Horticulture   ☐

Art & Design & Performing Arts   ☐

Tertiary   ☐

Designated   ☐

5   Does the college have a library?

Yes ☐

No ☐

If no, please return this questionnaire in the envelope provided.

6   Has the college been involved in a
merger within the last 2 years?

Yes ☐

No ☐

7   Is the college likely to be involved in a
merger within the next year?

Yes ☐

No ☐

8   What is the current position of the library within the college structure?

Autonomous ☐

Part of Learning Resources Department ☐

Part of Student/Client Services ☐

Other (*please describe*) ☐

....

9   What is the relationship of the Librarian or Head of Service with the Senior Management Team of the college?

Member in own right ☐

Reports directly to Senior Management Team member ☐

(*please give job title*) ....

Reports indirectly to Senior Management Team via someone else ☐
(*please give job title*)...

Other (*please describe*) ☐

....

10   Does the **library** or converged service have its own statement of aims/objectives, or a strategic plan or similar, which has been agreed with the college?

Yes ☐

In preparation ☐

No ☐

11   Does the **library** or converged service publish a users' charter/service level agreement?

Yes ☐

In preparation ☐

No ☐

LIBRARY SERVICES

12   Please show in
column a) how many sites the college operated from on 31 July 1994 and in
column b) how many of these sites offered **staffed** library services.

Number of sites	a)	Number of sites with staffed library	b)
1 site	☐	1 site	☐
2 sites	☐	2 sites	☐
3 sites	☐	3 sites	☐
4 sites	☐	4 sites	☐
5 sites	☐	5 sites	☐
6 sites	☐	6 sites	☐
Over 6 sites	☐	Over 6 sites	☐

13   What was the gross floor area occupied by
library services across all sites on 31 July 1994?

*Please insert the information either by sq m or by
sq ft or tick in the INR box if the information is not
recorded.*

	sq m
	sq ft

INR
☐

14   Please provide information about **total numbers** of the following aspects of provision within
the library on 31 July 1994.
*For each part of the question, please insert a number or tick in the INR box if the information is not
recorded.*

Aspects of provision	Total number across all sites	INR
Number of reader places		
Number of video playback facilities		
Number of audio tape recorders		
Number of slide projectors		
Number of photocopiers for student use		
Number of PCs for students for use with CD-ROM		
Number of other PCs for student use		

15   Please provide information about **stock** for the following categories **across all sites**.
For each part of the question, please insert a number or tick in the INR box if the information is not recorded. Please note that withdrawals should include missing books.

Stock type	Number of total stock on 31.7.94	I N R	Number of additions in 1993-94	I N R	Number of withdrawals in 1993-94	I N R
Books						
Periodical titles						
CD-ROMS						
Films / videotapes						
Audio tapes						

16   Which functions of the college library service were automated?
Please tick in the box where all or a significant part of a function was automated or where the function was automated at one or more site.

Functions automated at 31 July 1994

Acquisitions ☐

Cataloguing ☐

Circulation ☐

Short loans ☐

Public access catalogue ☐

Reservations ☐

Serials control ☐

Inter-library loans ☐

Access to information sources eg Dialogue, Datastar ☐

Management information ☐

Other *(please describe)* ☐

....

None of the library functions automated ☐

17   What were the total number of opening hours **per week across all sites** during 1993-4?
      Add the opening hours from each site together to obtain the total number.

      During term-time | |
      During vacations | |

18   What was the average number of visits **per week across all sites** in 1993-4?
      These figures may be difficult to provide for libraries without people counters.
      Estimates based on aggregate samples would be acceptable.

                                                          INR

      During term-time | | | |

      During vacation | | | |

      Total visits (*if breakdown* | | | |
      not known)

19   Please provide information about **all issues across all sites over 52 weeks**.

                                                          INR

      Average issues per week | | | |

      Total issues in the year | | | |
      1993-4

FINANCE

20   Questions in this section require financial information for 1993-4. For most colleges the
      financial year ran from 1 April 1993 - 31 July 1994. Please indicate which period the figures
      you will be providing refer to.

                   1 April 1993 - 31 July 1994   ☐
                   1 April 1993 - 31 March 1994   ☐

21   In 1993-4, who decided the size of the total library budget?
      Please give a job title and/or committee name or tick in the INR box if this information is not known.

      Job title ....   INR

      Committee name ....   ☐

22   How much input do you think the Librarian or Head of Service had into this decision?

          A great deal ☐

          Some ☐

          Very little ☐

          None at all ☐

23   In 1993-4 who decided the detailed breakdown and allocation of the library budget?

      The Librarian or Head of Service *(in consultation with library team if appropriate)* ☐

      The committee responsible for library services ☐

      A staff member in another department or service in the college ☐

      Other *(please specify)* ☐

      ....

24   Please provide information about the annual library expenditure in 1993-4 and anticipated expenditure in 1994-5.
Most Librarians or Heads of Service will have information about salary budgets. However, if you have to calculate salary budgets yourself, please remember to add 15% to cover employer costs.

Expenditure	Expenditure 1993-4	I N R	Anticipated expenditure 1994-5	I N R
Excluding salaries				
Including salaries				

25   Please provide information about the total annual library expenditure in 1993-4 and anticipated expenditure for 1994-5.

	Expenditure 1993-4	I N R	Anticipated expenditure 1994-5	I N R
On books and pamphlets				
On periodical subscriptions				
On CD-ROMS and local and remote databases				
Other learning resources				

STAFFING

26 Please give details for the person who was in direct operational control of the library on 31 July 1994.

Title .... Grade .... Gender (M/F) ....

27 Which of the following qualifications or memberships did this person hold?

Academic qualification at first degree level or
above in library and information science ☐

Academic qualification at first degree level or
above but **not** in library and information science ☐

Member of the Library Association ☐

Member or fellow of the Institute of Information Scientists ☐

Other *(please describe)* ☐

....

28 How many (FTE) posts did the library service have in the following categories on 31 July 1994?
Please include the person in direct operational control. Term-time only staff should be included as an appropriate FTE proportion.

Management posts (on management spine)

Professionally qualified library posts (on academic contracts)

Professionally qualified library posts (on other contracts)

Secretarial/clerical posts

Other posts *(please describe below)*

....

29 How many of the **professionally qualified library staff** or those in **management positions** in the library who were in post on 31 July 1994 held the following qualifications or memberships?

*Do **not** include the person in direct operational control.*

Academic qualification at first degree level or above in library and information science	
Academic qualification at first degree level or above but not in library and information science	
Member of the Library Association	
Member or fellow of the Institute of Information Scientists	
Other posts (*please describe below*)	

....

30 Still looking at the **professionally qualified library staff** or those in **management positions** in the library in post on 31 July 1994 please show the numbers in each grade, whether they were male or female and numbers of FTEs.

*Please **include** the person in charge.*

Grade	Number in grade	Number of		FTEs
		Male	Female	
Sc4-6				
SO1				
SO2				
PO range				
Lecturer				
Senior Lecturer				
Management spine				

Other scales
(*please describe below*)

31   How many of the **library support staff** who were post on 31 July 1994 held the following
      qualifications in library-related areas?

Qualification	Number of staff
City & Guilds	
BTEC	
SCOTVEC	
NVQs	

32   Looking again at **library support staff** in post on 31 July 1994, please show the numbers in
      each grade, whether they were male or female and numbers of FTEs.

Grade	Number in grade	Number of		FTEs
		Male	Female	
Sc1				
Sc1/2				
Sc2				
Sc3				
Sc4				
Sc5				
Sc6				

Other scales
*(please describe
below)*

COLLEGE INFORMATION

33   What was the total annual college expenditure for 1993-4?

Excluding salaries

Including salaries

34   What was the student population of the college on 31 July 1994?

Total student numbers

Numbers of full-time equivalent
(FTE) students

35   What was the staff population of the college on 31 July 1994?

Total staff numbers

Numbers of full time equivalent
(FTE) staff

If you are unable to provide the information for any of the questions in this section please give the following details for someone who will be able to do so.

This person will be contacted by a member of the research team.

Name   ....

Job title/department   ....

Telephone/extension   ....

THANK YOU VERY MUCH FOR YOUR HELP

LIBRARY ASSOCIATION GUIDELINES

Figures A to E provide illustrations of data in relation to critical indicators, with the Library Association guidelines (described below) inserted as reference lines. Percentage figures on either side of the line describe proportions of college libraries which meet and do not meet the guideline value.

RECOMMENDATIONS

The Library Association recommends that:

1. The library service should develop a mission statement, aims and objectives in line with the college's mission statement and information strategy. These aims should be developed by consultation involving librarians, library clients and senior managers.

2. The head of library services should hold a senior management position within the college in order that the library can contribute fully to the curriculum needs of the institution.

3. The design of the library allows for the full range of current library services and equipment and for easy adaptation or expansion to meet future needs.

4. The library has access to both capital funds and a reliable level of recurrent funding, to enable it to develop and maintain equipment based services on which its users depend to support their information needs.

5. The library be provided with sufficient space to meet the needs of its clients. This should be not less than $0.42m^2$ per FTE student with no less than $500m^2$ regardless of student numbers.

6. The library should provide study spaces in a ratio of at least one space per 10 FTE students.

7. Professional posts should be held by Chartered members of the Library Association.

8. All library posts should be graded according to the duties and responsibilities undertaken so as to attract and retain staff of the required calibre.

9. The number of library staff should not be less than 1 per 330 FTE students in large colleges and 1 per 200 FTE students in small colleges.

10.   Library staff development and training should be considered an integral part of the institution's commitment to quality.

11.   The library budget be not less than £26.00, at 1995 prices, per FTE student, excluding salaries and on-costs.

12.   Librarians with budgetary responsibility acquire appropriate financial skills and techniques.

13.   The library be accessible to the whole college community.

14.   The total size of the library stock should relate to the size of the college. A minimum number of 17 items per FTE student should be available in colleges with more than 2500 FTE students, with smaller colleges requiring a higher figure.

15.   The number of new items purchased per year should achieve a stock replacement period of 12-15 years.

16.   A full range of professional services should be provided by the library.

17.   All appropriate library functions are automated in order to provide a better service to clients and enhance management information systems.

18.   An induction and Information Skills training programme be available to all library clients.

19.   Senior college managers must ensure that the appropriate technical support and staff training is provided to support the operation of IT facilities in the library.

20.   That the librarian is involved in all decisions surrounding the introduction or development of all courses including franchised courses.

21.   Senior college managers support and encourage the library staff in their efforts to deal with discipline and behaviour problems.

22. All aspects of the library service should be evaluated on the basis of their ability to satisfy the stated or implied needs of library clients.

23. College librarians and senior college managers work together to develop a set of performance indicators to assist in the evaluation of services.

24. Libraries validate their services by means of inspection and feedback from service users and non-users.

25. Libraries market their services to clients, aiming to develop awareness of, interest in, desire for and convictions about the value of library services.

Figure A : Floor Space per Student FTE (refers to paragraph 5 - LA Guidelines)

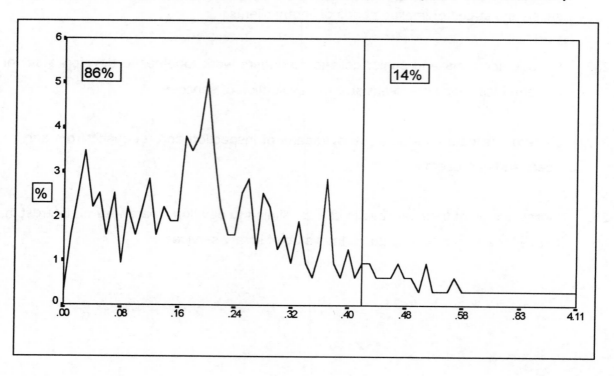

Figure B : Readers per Study Space (refers to paragraph 6 - LA Guidelines)

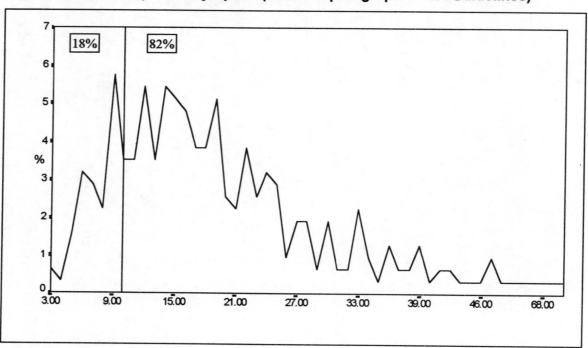

Figure C Library Expenditure (Excluding Salaries) per FTE Student

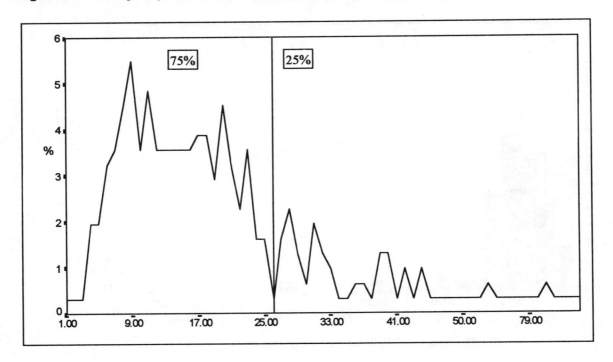

Figure D FTE Students per FTE Library Staff (Small Colleges)

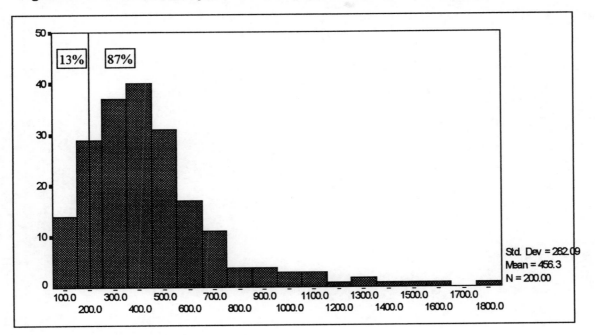

Figure E FTE Students per Library Staff (Large Colleges)

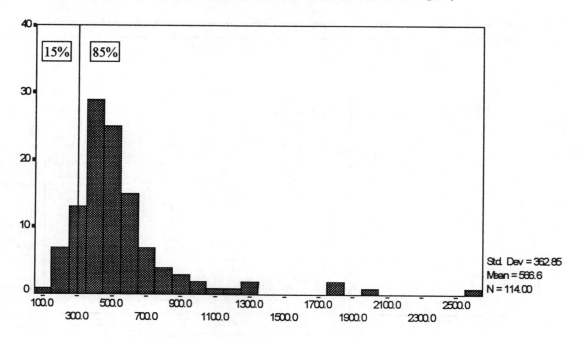

FTE Students per FTE Library staff (large colleges)

Std. Dev = 362.85
Mean = 566.6
N = 114.00

LIBRARY BUDGET INCREASES FOR PARTICULAR STOCK ITEMS

Table 5.17a   Book Budget Increase

% Increase	No of Colleges	%
< 0	70	26
0 < 20	50	18
20 < 40	58	21
40 < 80	54	20
80 +	38	14
Sample Size	**270**	**99**

Table 5.17b   Periodicals Budget Increase

% Increase	No of Colleges	%
< 20	94	35
20 < 40	73	27
40 +	104	38
Sample Size	**271**	**100**

Table 5.17c   CD-ROMs Budget Increase

% Increase	No of Colleges	%
< 20	67	32
20 < 40	42	20
40 < 80	34	16
80 +	67	32
Sample Size	**210**	**100**

INDICATORS OF PROVISION BY COUNTRY

Books per FTE Student By College Type By Country

Country	Sixth-form	GFE	Tertiary	Others
England	12.62	10.68	11.16	16.99
Wales	-	-	-	-
N.Ireland	-	7.01	-	16.76
Scotland	-	8.69	-	-

FTEs per Reader Place

Country	Sixth-form	GFE	Tertiary	Others
England	9.39	21.00	17.04	12.38
Wales	-	21.24	11.13	9.14
N.Ireland	-	32.97	-	11.51
Scotland	-	25.00	-	-

Library Expenditure (excluding salaries) per FTE Student

£	%			
	England	**Wales**	**N Ireland**	**Scotland**
< 10	22	27	45	32
10 - 15	20	9	11.13	32
15 - 20	17	27	0	21
20 - 25	16	18	0	0
25+	25	18	46	16
Sample Size	**268**	**11**	**19**	**11**

DETAILS OF INFORMATION NOT RECORDED (INR)

The INR box was provided in several questions to allow respondents to indicate that the information requested was not recorded, suggesting (though not conclusively) that information systems for these areas did not exist.

Question	No of colleges	%
Q.13 Floor area	107	
Q.14 Aspects of provision		
No reader places	5	
No videos	3	
No tape recorders	9	
No slide projectors	14	
No photocopiers	1	
No PC's with CD-ROM	2	
No other PC's	5	
Q.15 Stock		
Book stock at 31.7.94	21	
Periodical stock at 31.7.94	12	
CD-ROMs stock at 31.7.94	7	
Films/Videotapes at 31.7.94	37	
Audio tapes at 31.7.94	54	
Q.18 Visits per week		
During term-time	180	
During vacations	189	
Q.19 Issues		
Per week	71	
Total in year	72	
Q.21 Person/committee deciding budget	23	
Q.24 Expenditure		
Excluding salaries - 1993-4	8	
Excluding salaries - 1994-5	19	
Including salaries - 1993-4	106	
Including salaries - 1994-5	106	
Q 25 Stock Expenditure		
Books 1993-4	51	
Books 1994-5	56	
Periodicals subscriptions 1993-4	48	
Periodicals subscriptions 1994-5	51	
CD-ROMs and databases 1993-4	70	
CD-ROMs and databases 1994-5	78	

WITHDRAWN

HAVERING COLLEGE OF F & H E

17288